AVIATORS

Ruth Wolff

I0139493

BROADWAY PLAY PUBLISHING INC
New York
www.broadwayplaypublishing.com
info@broadwayplaypublishing.com

AVIATORS
© Copyright 2008 by Ruth Wolff

This play was first published by B P P I under the title BEYOND GRAVITY in September 2005.

First printing, this edition: December 2008
I S B N: 0-88145-424-9

Book design: Marie Donovan
Word processing: Microsoft Word
Typographic controls: Xerox Ventura Publisher 2.0 P E
Typeface: Palatino

A NOTE FROM THE PLAYWRIGHT

Although it comes in the guise of a living-room comedy/drama, AVIATORS is not a "realistic" play. The themes it deals with, however, are very real and very universal. Husband-Wife relationships. Father-Son relationships. Mother-Son relationships. Coming to terms with the Past. These are people trying to cope with the fact that life hasn't turned out as they expected it would. And I wonder how many people find themselves in that same situation. Dante said it best in the first Canto of his *Divine Comedy*: "Midway in the journey of our life I found myself in a dark wood, for the straight way was lost."

As the play begins we see people who have lost their way. They don't want to admit it, so they play games. Loving language, they sprinkle their banter with high and low literary allusions. Playing with words and ideas not only lifts them up, it helps them to avoid the abyss they are always circling. To suit their mood, I am as playful as they. I have deliberately used certain theatrical conventions—secrets, surprises—to lighten what becomes a deeper quest: How do you go on when you can't go on?

Gravity is the force that tries to pull you to earth—to pull you down. Going *beyond* gravity means exerting enough force not only to stand up against that force, but to actually triumph. Jan and Harry have different ways of standing against the force. Harry does it through wry humor and detachment, Jan by escaping into her imagination—imagining herself to be the wife of a hero (which was what, at the beginning of their marriage, she imagined herself to be). Projecting herself into another's life helps Jan to bear the traumas of her own.

I've always been fascinated by the mysterious relationship of marriage—why some marriages stay together and others break apart. The key is not just love, it's a congruent view of the world, a shared view of what life is about, what the goal of existence is, what are the things that matter most as one makes the inescapably hazardous journey. These qualities are what, it seems to me, the best marriages have—plus tremendous respect and admiration for each other *no matter what happens*. In lasting marriages there may be many crises which outsiders feel should tear the couple apart. But in the best marriages, *no matter what happens*, what holds the couple together is much stronger than what tears them apart.

In the action of the play a young stranger comes into Jan and Harry's lives—as listener, interrogator, understander, impartial judge and, finally, as delivering angel. She helps them to exorcise the past, conquer the present and face the future. She helps them to see what they have been unable, or unwilling, to see. She helps them to face truths. In my view, only by facing truths can we reach a level of revelation and resolution. In the twenty-four hour journey of the play, Jan and Harry discover truths about themselves and about their marriage. That is the kind of understanding which we can find in theatre. Fortunate are those who find that kind of understanding in their own lives.

AVIATORS was first produced by the New Jersey
Repertory Company (Gabor Barabas, Executive
Producer, SuzAnne Barabas, Artistic Director) in
association with Tina Chen. The play opened on 2 April
2005 with the following cast and creative contributors:

JAN HAWKESWORTH .... Gail Winar
HARRY HAWKESWORTH .... Peter Brouwer
FREDERICA .... Ellen Wolf

Director .... .Donald Brenner
Setting .... Carrie Mossman
Costumes .... Patricia E. Doherty
Lighting .... .Jill Nagle
Sound .... Merek Royce Press
Production stage manager .... Rose Riccardi

AVIATORS was subsequently produced at the Barter Theater, the State Theater of Virginia (Richard Rose, Producing Artistic Director). The play opened on 16 September 2005 with the following cast and creative contributors:

JAN HAWKESWORTH . . . . Tricia Matthews
HARRY HAWKESWORTH . . . . Eugene Wolf
FREDERICA . . . . Seanna Hollingsworth

Director . . . . John Hardy
Setting . . . . Derek Smith
Costumes . . . . Amanda Aldridge
Lighting . . . . Michael Nowack
Sound . . . . Bobby Beck
Production stage manager . . . . Karen N Rowe

To avoid confusion with a film of similar title which premiered at the same time, for these productions the play was called BEYOND GRAVITY. Its original title, AVIATORS, is now restored.

CHARACTERS

JAN HAWKESWORTH
HARRY HAWKESWORTH
FREDERICA

SETTING

Time: The present

Place: A room for living in a house poised between land and sea.

The sea is off, upstage right. The land is opposite, downstage left, out front beyond the invisible fourth wall.

Upstage right, tall glass doors open onto the sea. Nearby are a small dining table and two chairs. Upstage, near them, is a folding screen.

Center stage left is a sofa with a chair beside it. Behind the sofa is a table used as a desk, with a chair behind it.

Upstage center is an opening to a dimly-lit hallway. If one exits through it toward stage left, one goes out the front door. If one exits through it toward stage right, one goes into all the other areas of the house.

The house, provided by the college, is the home of academics, so the walls are entirely covered with bookshelves on which are books and papers—not in sets but in some measure of disarray. They are books which are used.

There is something about this space which moves away from realism. Is it the colors—all in monotone? Is it the fact the books are all covered in onion skin so they seem to blend into each other and become almost like wallpaper? Is it the mystery of the dark space of the hallway, into which people seem to disappear when they enter it? Is it the angle of the rafters—which gives a sense of the space being askew? There are no "extras" in the room—no bits of decor which are not used within the action.

The house is neither old nor new. Standing where it stands, alone, between the sea and the land, it has an atmosphere of both enclosure and exposure, of providing shelter but also of being vulnerable to invasion by land and by sea.

The action of AVIATORS takes place in two acts with one intermission.

ACT ONE

Scene One: The Hawkesworth Living Room.
A late afternoon in Spring
Scene Two: The next morning

ACT TWO

Scene One: Immediately following
Scene Two: Later that afternoon

For each of those special people whose friendship and support have meant so much to me over the years

ACT ONE

Scene One

(Time: The present. Late afternoon. Spring)

(Place: The Hawkesworth living room)

(At rise: JAN *is standing upstage right reading a book.* HARRY *is seated upstage left at the table, grading some examination booklets. Both academics, they are in their late forties or early to mid-fifties. The room is filled with the loud pulsating sounds of the sea.* JAN *listens to the waves breaking and receding. They are so loud she closes the book, looks out toward the sea through the glass doors and says:)*

JAN: Harry,—let's go for a walk!

HARRY: *(Busy with his papers)* Can't possibly.

JAN: Let's go for a swim!

HARRY: *(Holding up the exam books he has yet to correct)* Sorry. Can't.

JAN: But the sea is calling! Listen! ...What is the sea saying? Multiple choice: Swim me? ...Sail me? ...Clean me? ...Drown in me?

HARRY: None of the above.

JAN: What do you mean?

HARRY: I think that sound is not the sea. I think that sound is coming from the other direction.

*(*JAN *stops and listens for a moment.)*

JAN: So it is. I always said you had the best ears in the family.

(On the way to downstage left she passes him at the desk and kisses his ears. Then she walks downstage and looks out through the unseen window in the fourth wall.)

JAN: Good Lord! Look at all those people! What are they doing on the lawn? ...They're saying things. I understand them less than I understood the ocean.... They're waving things.

HARRY: Lengths of rope?

JAN: No, no, no! They're smiling. I think. God, I've never seen so many people!

HARRY: Are you sure that, whatever they're there for, it has something to do with us?

JAN: Who else? There's not another house around for acres.

(At last he puts his exam books down and comes to look out the window.)

HARRY: Well! That *is* a lot of people! Perhaps it's a convention of lemmings making their way to the sea.

JAN: Seems to me they're not so much making their way to the sea as congregating on our lawn.

HARRY: What are they waving?

JAN: Looks like papers. Newspapers.

HARRY: I think I see some kids from my classes.... Ah, yes. There's the wag from History 101 who's always trying to trap me with obscure questions about the rise and fall of the Roman Empire.

JAN: You know, I think I see a few of *my* more enthusiastic fledglings out there.... Oh, God. Yes! There's the joker from English Composition who keeps showering me with pornographic limericks!

HARRY: Is there any other kind?

JAN: If only his rhymed. Or had meter. Or made sense. They might actually be amusing.

HARRY: You'll have to recite some for me someday.

JAN: I promise you, if ever I recite to you pornographic limericks, they will be my own.

HARRY: Can't wait.

(They lightly kiss. Then)

JAN: I wonder what they're all doing out there, jumping up and down and waving things—and shouting something. What in the world are they shouting?

(The sound of the sea rises.)

HARRY: I think they're calling "Hawkesworth! Hawkesworth!"

JAN: *Jan* Hawkesworth or *Harry* Hawkesworth?

HARRY: Can't tell.

JAN: Have they come to praise us or to lynch us?

HARRY: Can't tell that either... Only one way to find out... *(He starts upstage to go toward the front door.)*

JAN: Don't! Don't go! I have an awful premonition—

HARRY: If there'd been any truth in any of your premonitions, we'd long ago have been dead.

JAN: There's always a first time—

HARRY: Perhaps. But I have a premonition this isn't it. *(Melodramatically)* If they eat me alive and throw my skeleton into the sea, you finish grading my exams, sweet.

JAN: I promise.

(HARRY exits.)

(JAN *turns to us and says*)

JAN: Harry was always braver than I. Smarter and braver. He has this solid way of looking at life. Clear. Right in the eye. He doesn't go up over hills and down into the valleys, as I do. He steers along, absolutely straight. No pebbles trip him up. No boulders block his road. Neither snow, nor rain, nor heat, nor gloom of night stops him from making his way through existence. He just surges forward, oblivious of all the pitfalls. Steady. Unsuppressible. While I—

(HARRY *returns. He is carrying a newspaper*)

Well?

HARRY: It seems that it *is* Hawkesworth they are chanting.

JAN: Yes, and—?

HARRY: And it seems the Hawkesworth they're shouting at the top of their lungs for—is you.

JAN: Me—?!

(HARRY *tantalizes her with silence for some seconds, then*)

HARRY: ...It seems you've won a Pulitzer.

JAN: What?!

HARRY: It's right here in the college newspaper. "Jan Hawkesworth Wins Pulitzer Prize for Poetry."

(*She looks at the paper.*)

JAN: That's crazy.... Excuse me, but that's crazy....
I published one volume. One very thin volume.
One very thin volume from a university press.
One very thin volume from a university press which sold maybe two hundred copies. One very thin volume from a university press which sold maybe two hundred copies all of them at this school. One very thin volume from a university press which—

HARRY: Okay, okay! What you say has truth, beauty, rhythm, granted no rhyme, and is not a limerick, and yet—here it is. And your subjects have come to congratulate you.

JAN: My goodness—!

HARRY: May we quote you, Madame? On receiving news that she had won a Pulitzer, Poet Hawkesworth cried: "My goodness!"

JAN: I'm speechless—

HARRY: That's rather inconvenient as I think your students and mine and the rest of the intellectual rabble out there are expecting a speech.

VOICES: *(From outside)*Hawkesworth! Hawkesworth!

JAN: Can't face the crowd without my hair combed—

HARRY: No, you're not that kind of poet.

JAN: Where's my comb? ... Oh, got it. *(She searches for her comb, finds it and combs her hair.)*

HARRY: Lovely. Now get out there—

JAN: Can't face the crowd without some lipstick. *(She searches for and puts on lipstick.)*

HARRY: Jan! How far is this dolling up going to go?

JAN: Can't face the crowd in this blouse—

HARRY: You could—

JAN: No. I couldn't. *(She goes off up right to change her blouse.)*

HARRY: *(To us)* This is a bit of a shocker. My wife. Jan. A Pulitzer Prize. Don't mean to be disloyal about my beloved's poetic capacities but they are, to put it bluntly, minor. I say so. She'd say so. Anyone who's read her would say "minor". She's dreamy, when the present world of poetry is sharp as a bayonet. She's

insubstantial. Given to flights of fancy. I keep telling
her: "Be precise. Be specific." She prefers to deal in air.
And—I don't mean to knock a major prize, but there's
the political aspect. You don't get the glittering prizes
unless they know you. They don't know you unless
you've blown your horn someplace where they can
hear. And outside of this—I can only say "minor"
institution—who has heard of Jan Hawkesworth? ...For
that matter, who has heard of *Harry* Hawkesworth?
...Our extreme anonymity mitigates against the major
medals—

(JAN *reappears, having changed her blouse.*)

JAN: Ah, yes. Very handsome, my dear. The perfect
costume in which to receive congratulations on a
Pulitzer. Not too casual, not too assumptive—

JAN: I had to sew on one of the buttons—

HARRY: Glad you did. Unbuttoned is unacceptable.
Particularly on national T V.

JAN: National T V!

HARRY: I glimpsed mikes from all the networks and
several cable channels in the crowd. I thought I'd better
warn you. You'll find tape recorders. Film and still and
television cameras. The works. Watch out, baby, they
want to grab your soul.

JAN: (*She checks herself in the mirror.*) One is never
prepared for such a thing. Could never be prepared
for such a thing. What if they ask me to quote a few
of my lines? I don't know any by heart! My brain's
total jelly! What if they ask me about our lives?

HARRY: You've lived them. You know what to say.
(*A beat*) ...What not to say.

JAN: Harry! I'm not ready!

HARRY: Jan, dear Jan—you are. *(He puts both hands on her shoulders.)* You are ready because, no matter what you may think, no matter how much, in bed at night, you've thought of yourself as an "obscure poet and always will be", you knew, in your heart, you deserved recognition. You create, not giant volcanoes, but tiny gems. Insightful, perfect, deep, mysterious, enchanting gems. The world is to be congratulated for noticing.... Go out and receive their congratulations. You already have mine.

(He kisses her lightly on the forehead.)

JAN: But *you're* the star in the family—

HARRY: Dearest Jan, go out and twinkle.

JAN: Come with me—

HARRY: No, sweetheart. The twinkling of this day is thine.

(He bows mockingly, formally. She smiles and exits toward the front door. When she has gone, HARRY goes to the window to observe what's happening and says to us)

HARRY: She was right to dress for the occasion. Whatever you're wrapped in as they snap you for the front page of *The Times* becomes iconic. If your hair happens to fall across your brow they call you windblown, though your tresses are usually impeccable. Intricacies of character are read into your threads. Diplomats don't want to give any clue to what they're thinking. That's why they all wear the same grey suit! Now Jan, as she appears before the multitudes is— *(Suddenly he looks surprised, puzzled, concerned. He is silent. Then he says to us, finally)* They're walking away! The whole crowd! Dispersing! Just as she got out there—they turned their backs and started walking away!

(JAN *re-enters, carrying a white envelope. She is walking slowly. Stunned*)

What happened?

JAN: It seems, my pet, there is another me! The prize goes not to a Jan, but to a *Janet* Hawkesworth!

HARRY: I never heard of her—

JAN: Apparently there's another obscure Hawkesworth minor poet! Just as I made my appearance someone in the crowd got the news on their cell phone and they've all departed to shout "Hawkesworth" on the lawn of this unknown but anointed Janet! ...Harry, what if I'd gone out there earlier? What if I'd presented myself to the public and the press and blushed and stammered and cast my eyes down modestly—and they'd ululated and cooed and fawned all over me—and then I had to watch them back off! ...What an ass I'd have made of myself!

HARRY: *You're* not the ass! *They* are!

JAN: I knew the news of such a triumph should come over the telephone, or in an envelope marked Special Delivery, Priority Mail. It doesn't come with assorted friends and strangers shouting your name on your front lawn.... My God! How humiliating! ...Are they all gone?

(He looks out the window.)

HARRY: All. Every one of them marked absent.

JAN: I have only one regret.

HARRY: Yes?

JAN: That I changed my blouse for nothing.

HARRY: Yes, but you sewed on a button. So you profited something.

JAN: Yes. I profited something.

(A silence. HARRY *looks at the envelope she's carrying.)*

HARRY: What's that?

JAN: Oh. I picked it up from the mailbox.... I thought it might be my official notification. *(She looks at it for the first time.)* No. It has your name on it.

(She hands it to him. He opens it. He reads it, then, expressionlessly, says)

HARRY: It's from President Cadwell. He wants to see me in his office.

JAN: When?

HARRY: Tomorrow morning.

JAN: Why?

HARRY: Doesn't say.

JAN: Perhaps he's ready to cut the size of your classes, as you requested.

HARRY: It doesn't say that.

JAN: Maybe it's about tenure.

HARRY: Doesn't say.

JAN: Perhaps he wants you to teach *Twenty-First Century Thought*—ideas for the future—the course you've been begging them to institute—

HARRY: There's no hint—. Just my name. The time. And the summons.

JAN: What time?

HARRY: Ten o'clock.

JAN: *(After a pause)* ...You don't think they've found out, do you?

HARRY: *(After another pause)* ...After all this time? I don't think so.

JAN: We've done marvelously so far—

HARRY: *(With concern)* Marvelously...

JAN: Who cares about what he might say? You don't have to be everybody's hero. You only have to be mine!

HARRY: Your hero? What have I done to deserve that appellation?

JAN: You know. My God, but you were splendid!

HARRY: Hero Guy. That's me! Killing the roach who moved into our kitchen. Unstopping the toilet when our plumbing was clogged—

(JAN brings out a small model of the Spirit of Saint Louis and holds it.)

JAN: Flying solo across the Atlantic! First one to do it—ever!

HARRY: "Flying solo across the Atlantic—!"

JAN: How I wish I could have flown that journey!

HARRY: So do I!

JAN: Do you wish you'd known me then? Do you wish you could have taken me with you?

HARRY: What I wish is that I could have done it!

JAN: But you did! Tell me again how you thought about it, dreamed about it, Lindy!

HARRY: "Lindy—!"

JAN: Tell me again how you made your plans so carefully. Checked the winds, checked the plane, checked the skies—

HARRY: Jan, darling, if you're going to pretend I'm somebody else, why not Beethoven? Why not Julius Caesar? Why not Elvis? *(He does a mock bump and grind.)*

JAN: Tell me again how you suited up—so tall and blond and handsome—

HARRY: Tall and blond and handsome. A combination devoutly to be wished.

JAN: I worshipped you for that. I still do.

HARRY: How about some dinner?

JAN: You never had the hungers that the world had. You were above that. You craved for more. The conquest of the sky—

HARRY: Jan, I don't want to play. I'm tired—

JAN: Not you. You're never tired. You are superhuman!

HARRY: *(Beginning to get annoyed)* Jan, for Chrissake—! Quit it.

JAN: Of course you were careful to a fault—because there's no use killing yourself—

HARRY: At this point I'm not so certain—

JAN: Why are you jettisoning everything, including your pen and your handkerchief?

HARRY: If I play, will I get to eat?

JAN: First you have to run the check list.

HARRY: You run it.

JAN: The pilot has to run it!

HARRY: *(Giving in reluctantly)* It's lucky I was an eagle scout—. Let's see— ... Ailerons— Check. Engine— Check. Propeller— Check. Roast chicken—

JAN: Stop it!

HARRY: Franks and beans?

JAN: If you don't run the check list correctly, you will not survive! Fasten your safety belt—

HARRY: *(Still with reluctance)* Fastening my safety belt.

JAN: Rev up your engine!

HARRY: Revving up my engine— *(He makes engine revving up noises.)*

JAN: Taxi down the runway. Take off!

HARRY: Taking off—

JAN: Careful of the wires! Under the wires—then up above the fog!

HARRY: You've got me taking off in fog?

JAN: It'll clear—

HARRY: I certainly hope so.

JAN: Altitude! Altitude! ...Isn't it great to be up at last— alone—and secure in your little cockpit?

HARRY: It is delicious to be secure in my little cockpit—

JAN: Isn't it glorious—up near the heavens?

HARRY: Glorious.

JAN: Keep your eye on the compass! Don't go off course! Over the ocean now. Night is falling. Stars are coming out.

HARRY: I am getting bored—

JAN: Don't fall asleep!

HARRY: Jan, I don't want to play any more! I'm tired! I have no idea why Cadwell wants to see me and I—

JAN: Stay awake or you'll crash! How does one feel in the moment between life and death? Does one meet God? Or does black nothingness replace one's being?

HARRY: Nothingness... *(Distracted, worried with his own concerns)* How does one feel on the brink of nothingness...

JAN: Pay attention!

HARRY: How can I pay attention? I'm flying blind!
I'm going to crash!

JAN: You're not. You're going to succeed—my hero,
my darling—

HARRY: For God's sake, enough! Stop now!

JAN: That you, the idol of the world, should want to
marry *me*! Little mousy me! That you should whisk
me above all the world and propose when we were
high above the clouds—

HARRY: Jan! In the name of heaven! Come back to earth!
Stop pretending to be Lady Lindy and look at me!

(She looks at him. She says, exceedingly normally)

JAN: Did you say you wanted dinner?

HARRY: No. I've lost my appetite. What happened to
you? What was going on with you?

JAN: What are you talking about?

HARRY: Never mind. *(He indicates the airplane.)* Where
did you get that?

JAN: This? I've always had it.

HARRY: I never saw it before.

JAN: You don't know everything about me. *(She puts the
airplane down on the table)* ...Shall I try to think up
something for dinner?

HARRY: No. I'm not hungry any more.

JAN: Neither am I. Let's go to bed.

*(He puts out the lights and they exit up right toward the
bedroom.)*

*(Shortly after they exit, a young woman appears outside the
glass doors stage right. She turns the handle and enters.*

Attractive and intelligent, she looks slowly around the room, observing everything. Her eye lights on the airplane. She picks it up, turns it in her hand, then puts it down again. She looks carefully around the room. Then she takes out a notebook and starts making notes.)

(Blackout)

(End of Scene One)

Scene Two

(The next morning)

(The young woman has fallen asleep on the couch. HARRY crosses the hallway past the upstage opening on his way out to get the paper. He doesn't see her.)

(The young woman hears the outer door slam. Hearing JAN about to enter from the hall, the young woman jumps up, straightens her clothes, picks up her notebook and starts toward the glass doors.)

(However, just as JAN enters from the hallway carrying two cups of coffee, HARRY appears outside the glass doors. Seeing no means of escape, the young woman hides behind the screen just as JAN comes into the room carrying two cups of coffee and HARRY comes in brushing sand off the newspaper)

HARRY: That paper boy is getting better and better at missing the porch completely. Today he managed to throw this halfway down the beach!

JAN: Coffee?

HARRY: Half a cup. I have to leave soon.

(JAN looks out of the downstage left window.)

JAN: No people...

HARRY: No people!

JAN: A blessing.

HARRY: A relief.

(They sit at the upstage right table by the glass doors.
HARRY *gives* JAN *a piece of the paper and they start to read.)*

JAN: This is how I like us best. Alone together... Don't
we have fun?

HARRY: *(Singing)* Every morning,
Every evening,
Ain't we got fun?

JAN: *(Singing)* Times are bum
And getting bummer
Still we have fun.

JAN & HARRY: *(Singing together in harmony)*
There's nothing surer
The rich get rich and the poor get poorer
In the meantime, in between time
Ain't we got fun!
(They laugh together.)

JAN: What *is* that?

HARRY: Tin Pan Alley Song. 1921. Lyrics by Gus Kahn
and Raymond B Egan, Music by Richard Whiting.

JAN: How much you know! Love that. Love you...
And I'm sorry you can't sleep.

HARRY: I sleep.

JAN: You didn't last night.

HARRY: I did.

JAN: You kept twitching.

HARRY: I didn't.

JAN: You did.

HARRY: I must have kept you up.

JAN: Not at all.

HARRY: If you'd been asleep, you wouldn't have been aware of my twitching.

JAN: All right. I was up.

HARRY: Then why didn't you say that?

JAN: What?

HARRY: That you didn't sleep. Instead you say *I* didn't sleep and we go through this whole rigmarole of your pretending to be worried that *I* didn't sleep when actually it's *you* who didn't sleep. Why do you pretend this is about me when it's about you?

JAN: Because it *is* about you. It's about your meeting this morning.

HARRY: You didn't sleep because of my meeting?

JAN: What's it going to be about, Harry?

HARRY: We've been through this—

JAN: You have some idea but you won't tell me—

HARRY: I don't.

JAN: You have suspicions. You're keeping mum.

HARRY: I've never been "mum". I am not "mum" now. If I had any idea I wouldn't be too shy to say!

JAN: I'm not accusing you of shyness, trepidation or timidity, I just want to know—

HARRY: In the name of heaven—!

JAN: Morning explosion number one! Do you notice how little it takes for an argument to ignite between us recently? We have the reputation on campus of being The Ideal Couple. They should see us now! I ask something simple like: "Do you know what

today's meeting with President Cadwell is going
to be about" and you go ballistic!

HARRY: "Go ballistic" is a cliché unworthy of a poet and
an authority on literature and the English Language.

JAN: That's a favorite trick of yours—when you can't
criticize my ideas, criticize my vocabulary!

HARRY: Your vocabulary is part Milton, part
prepubescent teen!

JAN: I'll say it very clearly, then, eschewing slang and
all words you might consider of unworthy provenance:
...Could it be over?

(Silence. Then he notices—the sun is in her face.)

HARRY: I know what the problem is: the sun is melting
your brain.

JAN: Harry, I'm asking you: Could it all, today, be *fini*?

HARRY: Do you want me to pull down the blind?

JAN: It's broken.

HARRY: Why don't you tell me these things?

JAN: What things?

HARRY: About the broken blind!

JAN: Oh, for God's sake, it's not about the blind, it's
about our survival!

*(HARRY starts to pull the screen in front of the glass doors
to shade JAN's eyes. The young woman is revealed. JAN and
HARRY are stunned)*

HARRY: What the devil—?

JAN: Who—?

HARRY: Who the hell are you?

JAN: What were you doing behind—?

HARRY: *(To* JAN*)* Call the police—

FREDERICA: Wait. Wait! I can explain—

JAN: Is she armed?

FREDERICA: Of course I'm armed.

(She reaches inside her bag. The others recoil. She pulls out a pad of paper and a pencil)

FREDERICA: My weapons. I have a license to carry them. I'm a reporter.

HARRY: For what paper?

FREDERICA: No paper. I'm free lance.

HARRY: Out—!

FREDERICA: When the others left, I stayed.

JAN: I can't imagine why.

FREDERICA: *(To* JAN*)* I love your work. I want to interview you.

HARRY: If you don't belong to a paper—

FREDERICA: When I've written it, I know I can get it published. *(To* JAN*)* Just let me talk to you—

JAN: To Jan Hawkesworth who is not *Janet* Hawkesworth? What would it be: "An Interview with Jan Hawkesworth—The Poet Who Did *Not* Win the Pulitzer Prize"?

FREDERICA: You should have won. You *could* have won. Your work—

JAN: —is completely unknown.

FREDERICA: That's my point. Why not make a virtue out of *not* being Janet Hawkesworth?

JAN: Portrait of a Loser.

HARRY: Our numbers are legion.

JAN: How did you discover my work?

FREDERICA: It was given to me by a friend.

JAN: But for you to print a story about a mistake—

FREDERICA: *(To* JAN*)* It'll bring you a public.

JAN: I *would* like the work to have a few more readers.
One does want to feel one isn't shouting into the dark—

FREDERICA: Then you'll do it—

HARRY: This is a bad idea—

JAN: Why?

HARRY: We have other things to do today! *(He looks at
his watch. His meeting is imminent.)*

JAN: *You* do. *I* don't. *(She turns to the girl)* What's your
name?

FREDERICA: Frederica.

JAN: *(Gesturing* FREDERICA *to a seat)* A pretty name.
Well, Frederica, what do you want to know?

FREDERICA: You were born—

JAN: Yes. Yes, I was. I was born. In a little town in the
East—

(As the interview begins and continues, under, HARRY *turns
to us and says)*

HARRY: Ah, the temptation of making revelations to the
press, which has entrée everywhere, and the vanity of
each of us, unable to resist reaching out for our fifteen
seconds of fame. What my wife wouldn't tell her
sister—if she had a sister—she will tell this woman.
What she wouldn't tell her best friend—if she had a
best friend—she would be happy to see in a six page
full-color spread in Keyhole Magazine—or even in one
paragraph on the next to last page of the last section of
the Daily Wigwag. It's a disease! Our need to show off!

Expose! Make every intimate detail of our lives public!
(He interrupts the interview. To JAN*)* I have to leave soon
and I think this interview should take place only in my
presence. So hurry up and get the story over with. Tell
it! Birth! Parents! Grandparents! School! College! Work!
Hubby! Hobby! Travel! Death! *(To us)* Is there anything
else to a life? Doesn't everybody's always serve itself
up in the same predictable courses? *(To* FREDERICA*)*
Tell me, are you after only the meat and potatoes—
or are you going to urge her to do a little more
creative cooking and spill out to you some of the
more intriguing ingredients of her mysterious sauce?
If you want to know the secrets of her sauce, ask *me.*

JAN: This is *my* interview.

HARRY: I know you—

JAN: You don't know me better than I know myself—

HARRY: Don't I? *(To* FREDERICA*)* Interview *me* about Jan
Hawkesworth. I know more about her than she knows
herself. More than she knows I know. More than she
would ever tell.

JAN: And I know more about you—!

HARRY: A draw!

FREDERICA: I would like to interview you, too, Professor
Hawkesworth.

HARRY: Ah, she knows I'm a professor—

JAN: *(To* FREDERICA*)* A considerably distinguished
one—. Protégé of the great historian Jonathan Stone.
The only one on earth worthy of inheriting Stone's
mantle.

FREDERICA: *(To* HARRY*)* Impressive... I would like to
interview you each separately—. But since you're here
together, perhaps I can ask the questions which relate to
you both.

JAN: Shoot.

HARRY: "Shoot"?

JAN: Isn't that what everybody says to reporters?

HARRY: I don't know what one says to reporters.
But if everybody says it, I wouldn't.

FREDERICA: Have you always worked together?
I mean in the same college?

JAN: Ever since we married.

FREDERICA: Which was how many years ago?

(Both answer simultaneously.)

JAN:	HARRY:
Twenty-six.	A century.

FREDERICA: You both taught at a college before this,
didn't you.

JAN: At an Ivy League institution whose name is so well
known it shall be nameless.

FREDERICA: And left it quite suddenly, so they say.
Why?

HARRY: We were offered a splendid opportunity at this
establishment—

JAN: And this house by the sea which we couldn't resist.

FREDERICA: How long ago was that?

JAN: Seven years ago.

FREDERICA: As I understand it, there was some pressure
for you to leave your former place of employment—

HARRY: Where did you get this information?

FREDERICA: Obscure corners of the web—

HARRY: That shallow sewer of misinformation! We left because they were trying to fence us in—and, for both of us, our interests had expanded.

JAN: My poems were beginning to be published. And Harry's articles were beginning to be published, too.

FREDERICA: I would have thought that would have made your presence at your previous institution even more valuable.

HARRY: I'm sure you're aware of the bitterness of academic jealousies. If you *half*-succeed, they praise you. But if you succeed too much, the knives come out to slice you to bits.

FREDERICA: That's why you left?

JAN & HARRY: Yes.

FREDERICA: But why in the middle of a semester?

HARRY: *(To* FREDERICA*)* Excuse me for interrupting the inquisition but are there going to be photos with this feature? Is my wife going to have her face scrutinized, air-brushed, color-toned? When you've done scratch-scratch, are you going to go click-click?

FREDERICA: I would like to. I didn't bring my camera.

JAN: Oh, *we* have a camera!

HARRY: One of those idiot-proof instruments where you can't fail—except, at the same time, you can never quite succeed.

FREDERICA: I'd be happy to take a picture if you—

JAN: Harry, why don't you get it for her?

HARRY: What?

JAN: I said—why don't you get it for her?

HARRY: I—

JAN: Go on. It's upstairs in the study. Go get it, Harry.

HARRY: *(He starts, reluctantly, to exit.)* Don't go too far in your confession! I will be able to hear— *(He exits into the house up right.)*

(When the women are alone)

JAN: He can't, you know. Hear. The camera's way off on the other side of the house. I apologize for my husband. He's in a mood. He has an appointment this morning—with the President of the College—

FREDERICA: On something crucial?

JAN: That's just it. We don't know. *(Troubled)* We don't know...

FREDERICA: Talking to me could help you keep your mind off things.

JAN: When you can't know the future, relive the past, is that it?

FREDERICA: Are you happy with your past?

JAN: *(Flatly)* Ecstatic.

FREDERICA: And your present?

JAN: *(Still flatly)* Ecstatic about the present, too.

FREDERICA: One thing I haven't asked—

JAN: What's that?

FREDERICA: About children.

JAN: What about them?

FREDERICA: Do you have any?

JAN: *(After a long pause)* No. No children.

FREDERICA: You didn't want them? Or you couldn't—? You tried and still you—?

(JAN gets out a worn and battered old-fashioned teddy bear.)

JAN: *(Holding the teddy bear, she is silent for a long time, then says)* ...We had a son.... But he was kidnapped.

(HARRY has entered just in time to hear this last. He thrusts the camera into FREDERICA's hands and says)

HARRY: Take her picture now. Why don't you take her picture? The light is just right. *(Indicating the teddy bear)* But first get rid of that thing—

JAN: No! *(Clutching it to her)* I still can't understand it. We all were in the house! You'd think we would have heard—!

HARRY: *(To FREDERICA)* Don't listen to her—

JAN: He was only two! Such a perfect child—! Asleep in his crib—! And they snatched him!

HARRY: *(To FREDERICA)* We never had a baby.

JAN: Snatched in the night from his second floor bedroom! I went in to gaze at him, to tuck him in again, and he was gone!

HARRY: Jan, this lovely young woman does not have to be treated to your ravings—

JAN: This is what came of my marrying the most famous man in the world!

HARRY: *(To FREDERICA)* She likes to exaggerate, my wife. I'm known in my field, but I definitely am not famous—

JAN: Reporters followed him everywhere. When my father, the Ambassador to Mexico, announced our engagement, it was front page news!

HARRY: *(To FREDERICA)* Her father had a shoe store north of Boston—

JAN: On the weekend when the press suspected we were going to be married, they staked out my parents' country house in New Jersey. Meanwhile, Charles and I—

FREDERICA: *Charles* and you—? I thought he was *Harry*—

JAN: Charles and I let the reporters catch a glimpse of us lolling about in ratty old clothes. We pretended we'd invited a few friends over for a cook-out. Instead, when everyone arrived, we got hitched!

HARRY: Jan and I were married in a Registrar's Office in Massachusetts—

JAN: What fun we had that day! Outwitting the reporters! Charles made a great show of having his plane ready and serviced at the air field—

HARRY: She totally discounts the fact that I get airsick—

JAN: Instead, we escaped to the sea and honeymooned on a yacht!

FREDERICA: A clever ruse. And when you returned, how did you manage to—

HARRY: *(To* FREDERICA*)* For heaven's sake, don't indulge her in this fantasy!

FREDERICA: Is it a fantasy?

HARRY: Poetic license. She is a poet, therefore flights of the imagination are required. Jan's flights allow her to escape from mental terra firma. It's a game she plays, sometimes for hours, the game of let's pretend.

FREDERICA: And in that time she cloaks herself in some other persona.

HARRY: Exactly.

FREDERICA: At the moment, she seems to be choosing to be Anne Morrow Lindbergh. *(To* JAN*)* If you can pretend to be anyone, why do you choose to be her?

JAN: You don't *choose* to be who you are. You *are* it. Inescapably!

FREDERICA: *(To* HARRY*)* I thought you said—

HARRY: She is pretending that she's not pretending.... My wife slips into new identities as easily as she slips into a new blouse.

JAN: You can't escape the glory. You can't escape the pain. I remember it as though it were yesterday. My first sight of the empty crib—

HARRY: Jan, please—

JAN: I went around the house, asking who had picked up the baby. But no one had him. We all hurried to the nursery. The window was open. None of us had opened it. There was a ladder propped up outside against the building. We knew, then, that our precious babe was gone.... *(To* HARRY*)* If only you had been anonymous—! In anonymity is safety!

HARRY: You're right. Forget this interview!

FREDERICA: Was there a ransom note?

HARRY: *(To* FREDERICA*)* Stop egging her on—

JAN: Of course there was a ransom note. Scrawled. In not good English—

FREDERICA: Whom did you suspect? The servants?

JAN: No matter how hard you check up on them, you can never be sure...

HARRY: Jan, this has gone far enough—. I really must get going—

JAN: *(To* HARRY*)* You shouldn't have tried to find the kidnappers yourself! You should have left things to the police!

HARRY: They're a bunch of bumbling clods! You do your best to point the way to truth then find that you yourself are under suspicion— ...What am I talking about! Now you've got *me* doing it!

JAN: *(To* FREDERICA*)* You can not imagine what it's like to love a thing so much—a little thing whose eyes look up at you with such trust, such unquestioning devotion, a little thing who puts his tiny life in your hands, to cherish and keep safe— *(She holds the teddy bear close and begins to keen back and forth.)* —a little thing which you have, and then, which you don't have. A thing you had once and loved with every fibre of your being—and which, in one day, is gone...

(As JAN *rocks to and fro, the baby in her arms,* HARRY *takes* FREDERICA *aside and says to her)*

HARRY: Whatever you do, you mustn't report this.

FREDERICA: She really seems to think she's Mrs Lindbergh.

HARRY: I told you—she's *pretending* she thinks she's Mrs Lindbergh.

FREDERICA: Is there a difference?

HARRY: Yes, of course. In one you're merely masquerading, in the other you're truly mad.

FREDERICA: And you think she's not mad.

HARRY: Jan mad? Impossible. You'd know if you'd lived with her for a hundred years as I have.

FREDERICA: But why is she doing it?

HARRY: Why do we all do what we do? Entertainment for an hour. Escape.

FREDERICA: But why *this* escape? Why the Lindberghs?

HARRY: Why not the Lindberghs?

FREDERICA: There were happier lives.

HARRY: Do you lead a happy life, Frederica? Do you have all you want? Or think you can one day have all you want? You're attractive. Young. Intelligent. *(Slightly suggestively)* Tell me, do you have all you want?

JAN: *(Observing them together)* Would you like me to leave so you and Frederica can have the living room alone together? Or perhaps the two of you would like to go upstairs—

HARRY: Don't be absurd—

JAN: I could go for a walk on the beach and leave you two to your own devices. I used to do that, did you know it, Harry? I used to pretend I wanted a long walk on the sand, when you were tutoring a student and I knew you wanted to be alone.

HARRY: Jan, quit this—!

JAN: *(To* FREDERICA*)* You're not so much beyond the age of one of Harry's students—

HARRY: I said stop it!

JAN: Of course the thing that Harry doesn't realize is— *I* had students, too.... Did you know that I had students, too, Harry? The great thing about teaching is that you always know each other's schedules. Always know when your mate is imprisoned in a classroom, always know when you can have the house to yourself—to do whatever you want.

HARRY: You don't have to go into—

JAN: Why not? Get out the yearbook. The yearbooks. I'll show you their pictures! *(To* FREDERICA*)* But there are worse betrayals than betrayals of the body—

HARRY: Enough, Jan! I beg you!

FREDERICA: Mrs Hawkesworth—

JAN: Mrs *Lindbergh.*

FREDERICA: Was it splendid? Flying with him, just you
two? In an open cockpit?

JAN: It was splendid! The wind blowing through my
hair—

HARRY: I would have thought your hair would be tight
inside an aviator's cap—

JAN: It was figurative! The wind blowing through my
hair is a figure of speech! It's what I need! What I must
have in my life! But you loved that, too, Lindy!

HARRY: *(Sardonically)* Yes. I loved it, Annie. Loved that
high flying with you. It's *this* high flying that's trying
my patience. I have to go see the President—

JAN: Calvin Coolidge.

HARRY: Ebenezer Cadwell.

JAN: Heads of State begged to have their pictures taken
with Lucky Lindy. Before he hurries off, come snap
a picture of Lindy and me. Go on. Go ahead. Take a
picture of the woman and her hero—

(JAN *takes* HARRY's *arm.* FREDERICA *starts to point the
camera at them)*

HARRY: No! Enough of this nonsense!

(He grabs the camera away before she can shoot.)

JAN: Forgive my husband. He gets tired of having
his picture taken. It steals the soul, you know.
And I suspect he feels that now his soul is gone.

HARRY: I have to go to this meeting! I have to be
composed! Somehow have my wits about me.

JAN: Isn't it odd how upset my dear husband can get
at the thought of a little meeting, when, in the defining

moment of our married life, he showed absolutely no emotion?

FREDERICA: And what do you consider the defining moment of your married life?

HARRY: No! Don't tell!

JAN: When they took our baby!

(HARRY, *expecting another response, is almost relieved.*)

JAN: When we didn't know what happened to him for days and days!

HARRY: *(Wearily)* We never had a baby.

JAN: I thought I might die, or go insane, or rip the flesh from my living body—but you went through the days like an uninvolved detective, sifting clues, winnowing possibilities, weighing ideas.

HARRY: Will you, for God's sake, cease and desist from this so I can go to my meeting with a clear head?

JAN: But you had a clear head. A totally clear head, when what was called for was to scream with horror! When they found my baby's body—

HARRY: You never had a baby!

JAN: You went to see it, identified the body from its little teeth and didn't even cry!

HARRY: *(Putting on his jacket)* I have to go—

JAN: And even when I slept with another man, you stood like a rock. Immutable.

FREDERICA: Anne Morrow Lindbergh slept with another man?

HARRY: *(Coldly)* Jan Hawkesworth slept with another man. She thought I didn't know. I knew.

JAN: You could not be moved. Even then. *(To*
FREDERICA*)* He is a rock, my husband. Emotionless.
Inhuman. But I understand it. If he allowed me a
dalliance, it was because he had deeper guilts of
his own.

HARRY: You'll excuse me. Frederica. Jan—or Anne—
whoever you are. I have to go. *(To* JAN*)* But remember
this: there are things we have never said that need
never be said. About which we swore to each other
we'd be silent forever.... And further remember:
anything you say to this young woman you could find
published on the front page of a tabloid newspaper—in
bold black type. *(He goes out the front door.)*

*(*JAN *and* FREDERICA *are alone)*

FREDERICA: He doesn't trust the press.

JAN: He has every reason.

FREDERICA: People who don't trust the press usually are
hiding something. Are you hiding something?

JAN: That's a very direct question.

FREDERICA: I find sometimes one gets further with
direct questions.

JAN: I am not hiding any more than most married
people hide on their main subject.

FREDERICA: Oh? And what is their main subject?

JAN: Their relationship. The nature of their relationship,
of course.

FREDERICA: And yours is not what it seems?

JAN: What does it seem?

FREDERICA: It seems—special.

JAN: Yes. I think it is.

FREDERICA: Able to stay steady through the storms—

JAN: You mean, you think tragedy would bind a special couple like us together.

FREDERICA: I would think so.

JAN: It did just the opposite. It tore us apart.

FREDERICA: What tragedy are you talking about? The kidnapped baby?

JAN: No. Not the kidnapped baby.

FREDERICA: What, then?

JAN: *(Sits and says:)* ...There are some tragedies which are too deep for words.

FREDERICA: In spite of the prickly veneer and the bantering discord, you two seem to have an absolutely unseverable bond.

JAN: An illusion. Everything you see before you is an illusion.

FREDERICA: What's the reality?

JAN: The reality is I didn't win the Pulitzer. The reality is the man I married is exactly like a stone. The reality is I have no son.

FREDERICA: Actually, I know you have a son, Mrs Hawkesworth. I'm married to him.

(JAN, *speechless, stares at* FREDERICA.)

(Blackout)

END ACT ONE

—

ACT TWO

Scene One

(Moments after the preceding scene. JAN has gotten up, paced excitedly and now asks FREDERICA:)

JAN: How is he? How is Adam? Is he well? Where are you living? Is he fine?

FREDERICA: He's very well. We live—only about an hour away from here.

JAN: Only an hour... Are you really a reporter?

FREDERICA: I am really a reporter. This, I'm afraid, is one assignment to which I wasn't assigned. I hope you don't mind. There won't be a printed interview—

JAN: I'd rather have a daughter-in-law than a thousand lines in any paper.

FREDERICA: I just wanted to know you. I was sorry that Adam wouldn't let me invite you to the wedding.

JAN: When was it?

FREDERICA: Two years ago.

JAN: Was it a big affair?

FREDERICA: Very small. Adam isn't, as you know, much of a crowd person.

JAN: Yes. He liked a pared down life. Parents, it seemed, took up too much room in it.

FREDERICA: Why do you and your husband pretend to have no son?

JAN: It makes things simpler. Adam left us before we came here. Slammed the door and said he never wanted to see us again. Ever.

FREDERICA: Did you never try to contact him—?

JAN: Of course I tried. In the beginning. But he refused to respond. He decided we did not exist so, when we got here, we decided *he* didn't. It was easier than explaining. I'm surprised he let you know we were still on this earth.

FREDERICA: He did at first tell me he was an orphan. But eventually he admitted you were alive.

JAN: So kind.

FREDERICA: What caused the rift?

JAN: He didn't tell you?

FREDERICA: He won't talk about it.

JAN: Discreet. Silent and discreet. Impenetrable. That's Adam.

FREDERICA: I've never found him impenetrable— except, perhaps, about this.

JAN: What's he doing?

FREDERICA: Writing.

JAN: Ah, the family curse.

FREDERICA: He writes well.

JAN: What is it? A novel? Dealing, as all first novels do, with his early life more or less in disguise?

FREDERICA: I don't know. He doesn't want me to read it until it's finished.

JAN: We shall be exposed, his father and I.... When he talks to you what does he say about us?

FREDERICA: Aside from that time he admitted you were alive, he never mentions you.

JAN: And yet you came.... How did you find us?

FREDERICA: There aren't that many Hawkesworths who are both professors. It was easy.

JAN: So you looked us up and came by to check us out.

FREDERICA: I wanted to see—

JAN: What we are. Who we are. If his silence about us hides a house of horrors.

FREDERICA: I never thought that.

JAN: Whatever made you come, I'm glad—so very glad—you did. After a while, one has a yearning for family. To have more family than I suspected pleases me more than I can say.

FREDERICA: Thank you.

JAN: I miss Adam. A lot. But Harry won't let me speak about him. Tell me more. Tell me everything. Tell me how you met and how you came to love each other. Tell me—

(She hears HARRY *coming into the house. Even before he enters the room she is calling—)*

JAN: Harry! Harry! We have a daughter! Frederica is our daughter!

*(*HARRY *enters. He looks unsettled—like a man who has heard bad news.)*

HARRY: We have no son, but suddenly we have a daughter. And fully grown. What a miraculous event! Did you give birth to her sometime when I wasn't looking? Or did you just adopt her in the past half-hour?

JAN: She's married to Adam.

HARRY: Who's Adam?

JAN: *(To* FREDERICA*)* You see? He's been erased. Harry refuses to remember. *(To* HARRY*)* Harry. Frederica knows he exists. She and Adam are married.

HARRY: I'm not going to say I have a son just because he married. He cut out of here. As far as I'm concerned, that was a final goodbye.

JAN: Harry—

HARRY: You don't ask how it went.

JAN: What went?

HARRY: My interview with the President. You don't ask what he wanted.

JAN: For each of us to take on extra classes?

HARRY: No.

JAN: For you to chair the history department again?

HARRY: No.

JAN: What then?

HARRY: *(A look at* FREDERICA, *then*—*)* He wants us out.

JAN: Wants us to leave the faculty?

HARRY: Leave the faculty, leave the school, leave the house.

JAN: *Why?!*

HARRY: Why leave the house? They're demolishing it to put up a gym, he says. As he points out, they own the house, they can do whatever they want with it. And what they really want—on this very spot of land, is a gymnasium. A gymnasium by the sea.

JAN: When does he want us to leave?

HARRY: Immediately.

JAN: *Now—?!*

HARRY: This afternoon. He claims they put a notice in our box some weeks ago. I claim he's lying. However, the wreckers will be here at any moment, so—

JAN: This is impossible—!

HARRY: They're shovelling us out, kiddo. Take what you think you need and let's go.

JAN: This is ridiculous! They can't—!

HARRY: That's life, my pet. Either there are crowds on the lawn waiting to shout your praises and carry you in triumph on their shoulders—or there are bulldozers on the lawn waiting to shovel you out.

FREDERICA: I don't understand. They may want to demolish your house. But why do they want you off the faculty?

HARRY: *(He hesitates a moment, then)* ...Something from the past has suddenly reared its ugly head and bit us.

JAN: What are you saying?

HARRY: *(To JAN)* I need to talk to you in private. Something has happened. Something this new daughter of yours—

JAN: —ours—

HARRY: —doesn't have to know.

JAN: Frederica can hear everything. She's family. We can be open with our family. Whatever it is, Frederica can know.

HARRY: ...All right. *(A pause, then he says, to both of them)* It seems—I've killed a man.

JAN: What—!

HARRY: To be more precise—I've killed him again.

JAN: What do you mean you've killed him again?

FREDERICA: I don't understand. How can you kill someone twice?

HARRY: You're young, Frederica. You don't know this yet: the worst murder isn't killing someone outright. The worst murder is if you wound them mortally but then they linger. And then, one day, when you've come to believe they're no longer a threat, they suddenly rear up and, just as they die, kill you.

JAN: What are you saying?

HARRY: I am saying that Jonathan Stone is dead. Killed himself. That's the news that President Cadwell summoned me to his chambers to impart to me. Jonathan Stone killed himself.

JAN: Oh—!

HARRY: Shot himself—

JAN: Where?

HARRY: Where did Jonathan Stone shoot himself? You mean in the heart? In the head? In the foot? He shot himself in the bathtub! He was so fastidious. Wouldn't you know if he had to shoot himself he'd do it in the bathtub—to make it easier for people to clean up after him.

JAN: *(Musing)* So Stone was not a stone after all...

FREDERICA: Is this the Jonathan Stone whose mantle you inherited?

HARRY: Whose mantle I *was* to inherit.

JAN: A man historians worshipped like a god. When Harry was a graduate student Stone was his mentor. He

was the one who taught Harry how to look at the past
and see what really was. *Without Professor Stone—*

HARRY: I have always credited him with my
success—such as it is, such as it was. Always!

FREDERICA: But what has his demise to do with you?

HARRY: The old professor left behind a farewell epistle.

JAN: A suicide note?

HARRY: Oh, much longer than a note. A six page letter
which he E-mailed to President Cadwell yesterday—
apparently just before he pulled the trigger.
(Interrupting himself. At the window) Oh, look!
The bulldozers are arriving. How shiny they are!
New brooms—to sweep us out clean...

FREDERICA: What happened back then? How long ago
are you talking about?

JAN: We're talking about when Stone had just retired
and Harry had taken his place on the faculty.

HARRY: *(To* FREDERICA*)* After he retired, Stone
published a book summing up his years of pondering
the history of human civilized life. *The Times Literary
Supplement* asked me to review it.

JAN: The editors knew Harry had been Stone's disciple.
It was clear they expected him to heap his old professor
with praise.

FREDERICA: *(To* HARRY*)* But you wrote a negative
review?

JAN: A very negative review.

HARRY: It was a review as honest and straightforward
as I could make it. His theories were completely
untenable!

FREDERICA: You'd learned from him—

HARRY: Yes. But these ideas he'd kept to himself.
In order to publish them for the first time in his great
summing-up volume.

JAN: In any case, in words quite unmistakable—
Harry skewered Stone's magnum opus.

HARRY: I told the truth! His theory was so bleak it
couldn't be borne! ...In this book Stone said that
humans are and always will be motivated primarily
by malice—a deep-seated desire to cause others pain!
It grieved me more than I can say to have to hurt the
man who had nurtured and encouraged me. But I could
not, in all honesty, let his theory stand!

FREDERICA: And this one negative review destroyed
Stone's reputation?

JAN: Oh, it wasn't only that. It was that, in his review,
Harry felt compelled to point out that several
paragraphs of Stone's huge volume had been lifted
word-for-word from earlier works.

HARRY: What should I have done? Ignored the fact
that—

JAN: You could have exercised a modicum of
compassion—I told you—

HARRY: (*To* FREDERICA) She thought I shouldn't have
pointed out the plagiarism—

JAN: (*To* FREDERICA) I thought, in the name of mercy,
he should have let the paragraphs go—

HARRY: The paper was testing me!

JAN: Nonsense! None of them knew. The passages were
too obscure. You told me you'd just happened—by
chance—to come upon the old volumes in which these
passages appeared a few months before reading his
book.

HARRY: Yes. By chance. By total chance.

JAN: It's likely no one else on earth could have made that discovery.

HARRY: No one— *(To* FREDERICA*)* But once I realized what he'd done, what was I to do?

JAN: *(To* FREDERICA*)* He could have chosen clemency. I begged him— *(To* HARRY*)* I begged you to act with leniency and grace and give him a pass—

FREDERICA: Perhaps the professor forgot these were paragraphs he knew by heart rather than invented.

HARRY: It doesn't matter how he came to do it. Once I noticed what was blatant plagiarism I couldn't ignore it! It wasn't just *his* career that was on the line, it was *mine.* If there'd been just *one* double-dome to point out that I'd missed such a thing—I would have become the laughing-stock of my profession.

JAN: *(To* FREDERICA*)* And so he told on his old professor.

HARRY: It tore me apart—!

JAN: *(Cynically)* Oh, yes—

HARRY: But I had to!

JAN: "You had to!" *(To* FREDERICA*)* For years Stone had taken Harry under his wing, shared his wisdom with him, encouraged him, groomed him, confided in him, made sure all along the way that Harry was promoted to the next rung of every ladder. And then, when it was Harry's turn to repay all of Stone's trust and friendship, Harry turned on him.

HARRY: I was doing exactly what Stone always taught me to do: I was being honest!

JAN: Your review shattered Stone's reputation! You reduced to nothing the sum and substance of the thinking of the man's entire life!

FREDERICA: What happened?

HARRY: Rather than congratulating me for my intellectual honesty, the faculty saw me as a traitor.

JAN: Harry and I were shunned. Colleagues turned away when we walked across the campus.

FREDERICA: They shunned both of you?

JAN: I stood by him. That's what a wife does, doesn't she? You don't desert the ship just because you hit rough seas.

FREDERICA: When the Professor read Harry's review, how did he respond?

JAN: By withdrawing from the world completely. He retreated into the hills. His young wife left him— this former student with her enviable combination of brains and beauty—left him. Stone went silent. Until yesterday, when, it seems, he blew his brains out.

HARRY: His entire life he had suicidal tendencies! The perfect life or self-annihilation! It was always his position!

JAN: And so the old professor shot himself—. *(She turns to HARRY.)* But not, apparently, before sending Cadwell a letter which somehow implicated you.

FREDERICA: But that review—it must have come out years ago. How many years ago was it?

JAN: Seven.

FREDERICA: When Adam left you—

JAN: Yes. When Adam left us. He judged us both— and his judgment was severe.

HARRY: Like our colleagues, Adam saw my honesty as betrayal. Like them, he decided to treat us as if we didn't exist.

JAN: We lost our jobs—and our son—at the same time.

FREDERICA: But why, if this happened so far in the past, did it take seven years for Jonathan Stone to kill himself?

HARRY: *(At the window, trying to distract from the conversation)* The shovels are moving into position—!

JAN: Murderer!

HARRY: It was not my fault!

JAN: So many died. So very many died...

HARRY: I went through hell knowing how hard it would hit the old professor—but the only path was the path of intellectual truth!

JAN: Herded into box cars!

HARRY: Hearing that he exploded his brain with a bullet leaves me suffering the tortures of the damned!

JAN: Marched off into gas chambers—

FREDERICA: *(To* HARRY*)* But why are they blaming you for his suicide? Had you been in touch with him recently?

HARRY: Since that incident? Never.

JAN: Killer! People were shoved into furnaces and when the flames died all that was left was charred and steaming bones.

HARRY: *(To* FREDERICA*)* Go to the window. See if more equipment has arrived— *(To* JAN*)* Jan, listen to me. We have to organize—

*(*FREDERICA *looks out.)*

FREDERICA: There are two bulldozers, a wrecker's ball and a dump truck. Those machines—they are enormous!

JAN: People burned to bits! And it was my husband's fault—my adored husband—standing on podiums telling everyone that Hitler was a savior!

HARRY: Oh, God, has she slipped back again? Am I suddenly, once again, tall and blond?

JAN: Traitor! Betrayer! Betrayer of our country. Betrayer of me.

HARRY: Jan, don't do this. Please. I beg you—

JAN: Once you had vision. Once you could see. Your flights—higher and faster and farther than anyone—gave you perspective no one else had. And instead of seeing true and using your fame to fight for people to be free to live in dignity and peace, you—

HARRY: (To FREDERICA) What am I going to do? She's driving me crazy!

FREDERICA: Perhaps if you humor her—

HARRY: I can't bear to see her this way—

FREDERICA: Why don't you play along. Pretend. It may help her to get over whatever it is that's troubling her.

JAN: You should have had some sympathy for those your actions ended up destroying!

HARRY: All Lindbergh ever said was that Hitler had superior military forces! That was a clear-eyed honest unflinching appraisal! As was my appraisal of Stone's book!

JAN: You should have known the horror that would result from your words—but you were blind! Went everywhere making speeches—tall and blond and beautiful—making speeches—saying we had nothing to fear from the monster. That he had made you promises. That there would be no war—

HARRY: No one can know in advance the consequences of one's actions—

JAN: You liked them, didn't you, those Germans. You thought they were so smart! Those uniforms. Their sense of order. Just like your sense of order. They had what you admired most—precise unsentimental minds!

HARRY: Their planes were better than our planes. They had enough air power to win!

JAN: They were fighting for a bad idea! But you didn't care, did you. You loved them! My hero. Seduced by the glamor of the Luftwaffe.

HARRY: I wanted peace!

JAN: You didn't care that innocents were being slaughtered—

HARRY: I made an objective judgment!

JAN: People died because of you—

HARRY: Lindbergh didn't know about the camps—

JAN: *(To* FREDERICA*)* You see how vain he is? Referring to himself in the third person? *(To* HARRY*)* People died because of you. Where was your sense of compassion? Where was the humanity I always believed was behind your cool impassive eyes? Where was your sense of the holiness of each and every life—?

HARRY: I did what I thought was right!

JAN: People died!

HARRY: Jan, in the name of God, I am not Lindbergh! I don't have to defend a man for how he lived his life! You're going mad and somehow I've become the enemy! Come out of this tailspin! I need you to be sane!

FREDERICA: *(At the window)* The bulldozers are moving closer.

HARRY: We're under attack on every side! I need you to hold steady!

JAN: How does it feel to have killed, my hero? How does it feel to have destroyed all those lives?

HARRY: One life. Perhaps one life!

JAN: Every life is connected to all other lives. When you kill one, you kill all the others.

HARRY: I called it as I saw it!

JAN: Jonathan Stone died for the way you saw it! Died in an oven!

HARRY: He shot himself in a bathtub!

JAN: Stone died in an oven because you stood on a platform and said Hitler was superb! You stood on a platform and let him annihilate millions!

HARRY: I wrote a negative review which pointed out that Jonathan Stone had copied several paragraphs—!

JAN: There must have been something more if they're condemning us now. *What is it?*

HARRY: There's nothing.

JAN: Betrayer! You betrayed your country, you betrayed Stone and you betrayed me!

HARRY: *(To* FREDERICA*)* Are you taking this down? It's poppycock! Drivel! You are witnessing insanity. A profound slippage of the mind—

JAN: After his betrayal, everything went bad. We were both let go from our jobs. It was hard to find a perch. Only this brain-forsaken place would take us. And our son left home. When he saw what his father was—and what I seemed to condone—he left. Slammed the door and never once looked back. Never called. Never told us he was married. *(To* FREDERICA*)* What Harry did is tantamount to murder, isn't it?

FREDERICA: I can't judge—

HARRY: You can. You must! You can't stay neutral!
Tell her that my hands are clean!

JAN: Assassin!

HARRY: *(To* FREDERICA*)* Do you think that I should have
her put away?

JAN: *(To* FREDERICA*)* Don't you think that he should be
punished—for all he caused to die?

HARRY: *(To* FREDERICA, *at the end of his rope)* What
should I do?

JAN: *(To* FREDERICA*)* Should I have left him? Should I
leave him now? We have five surviving children—

HARRY: We have no children—

FREDERICA: You have a son—

HARRY: If he disowned me, I disown him! Ties of blood
come untied if the rift is as wide as ours is.

JAN: How do you go on loving a man who was your
hero when he is no longer a hero? How do you go
on living, when that love was the center of your life?
...What should I do? Should I leave—?

HARRY: My God, go! I can't stand the madness any
longer! The bulldozers are moving in. We've been fired.
Don't you understand? They've let us go and they're
shovelling us out. Me because I'm the man whose
standards were so high he caused another's self-
destruction. And you because you stuck with me and
stayed silent—which showed that you approved.

JAN: I did not approve. I put the sacredness of my
marriage above my principles.

HARRY: The more fool you. I'm sorry for you, that in
your faith in me you were so self-deceived.

JAN: I can still leave you—

HARRY: Too late. There is a tide in the affairs of men—and women—which, taken at the flood—. But your flood tide has come and gone, my darling. Come and gone and left you beached on this very dry and arid shore. *(To* FREDERICA*)* You're not taking notes.

FREDERICA: I think—all this—should not be written.

JAN: Should it be told?

FREDERICA: To Adam? I don't know. I didn't tell him I was coming here to see you.

JAN: Why did you come?

FREDERICA: I came to see what Adam was running away from. You can't understand another until you can understand their past.

HARRY: The past can never be totally understood. I'm a historian and I say so.

FREDERICA: Even what can be glimpsed by the light of a match is helpful.

JAN: And have we helped you to see?

(The sound of the motor of a bulldozer)

HARRY: Excuse us. We're about to be scooped up and thrown into a dump truck. We have to pull together our few valuables, such as they are.

JAN: My book of poems. His white silk aviator's scarf—

HARRY: Oh, yes. My white silk aviator's scarf. With which, if the occasion demands, we could both hang ourselves.

FREDERICA: Adam's expecting me. But I could stay— I *should* stay—

JAN: Oh, no. This should not be witnessed.

FREDERICA: I could stay and help you pack—

JAN: It's good of you to suggest. But no. You couldn't tell what few things we value—

FREDERICA: *(Touching the airplane and the teddy bear)* Actually, I think I could.

JAN: Take them.

FREDERICA: No. They're yours.

HARRY: *(Gently)* Please. Go now...

FREDERICA: *(As she starts to go)* I'm glad I came. Even if we never see each other again, I'm glad we saw each other. I hope things will work out well for you.

JAN: Give our regards to—

(On a warning look from HARRY, JAN stops and is silent)

FREDERICA: *(At the exit, turning back, she says)* Perhaps you'd like to know— ...I'm carrying your grandchild.

(FREDERICA exits)

JAN: *(Joyously)* She's carrying our grandchild! There'll be another—

(The roar of the bulldozer gets louder.)

HARRY: Another Hawkesworth or another Lindbergh?

(The mechanical roar gets louder and louder.)

(Blackout)

(End of Scene)

Scene Two

(Later that afternoon)

(HARRY, alone, is upstage right at the glass doors looking out toward the ocean. He doesn't find what he is looking for. He turns to us and says)

HARRY: Jan went for a walk on the beach two hours ago and hasn't returned. That's not like her. Can't see her. She doesn't usually go out of sight of the house. *(He crosses the room and looks out the downstage left window)* Momentary quiet. The wreckers are taking their afternoon break. A small crowd has gathered. To watch the walls come tumbling down. Are they the same ones who yesterday came to praise? Have they returned today to see us reduced to rubble? *Sic transit gloria mundi... (He returns to peer out the upstage glass doors.)* Why doesn't Jan come back? I wonder if she's gone forever. Perhaps she walked into the sea. It would be just like her to end it with stones in one pocket and a copy of Virginia Woolf in the other. The coward's way out! ... No. Walking into the ocean is the essence of brave. As one walked in deeper and deeper there'd have to be tremendous will to fight the instinct to keep one's head above the water, to not struggle against going under.... What if the waves refused to take you? What if they screamed "No!" and buoyed you up and cast you onto the beach—humiliatingly alive.... No. The waves don't care if you want to float or if you want to drown. To them it makes no difference. Live or die, it makes no difference.... Goddam it, Jan, where are you?! *(He starts to open the door to go out then stops himself.)* Oh, what the hell! If that's what you want to do, do it! I won't stop you. God knows you have every reason. Now that we've come to the end of the line. *(He comes into the room.)* If she's done it, I ought to

have the courage to do it, too! One always has it at
the edge of one's mind—self-destruction. We all are
Hamlets under the skin, wondering whether to be or
not to be. It's not whether or not we want to exit—
it's how to do it that's the question. By the time you've
figured it out—and assembled the instrument that will
help you on the road to kingdom come, you feel it's
so much bother you may as well live a little longer....
My God! What if she's actually seen it through!
Actually chosen to go by water! What if, even now,
she's being tossed up on the shore, bloated and blue—!
*(Suddenly panicked, he starts rushing upstage right toward
the glass doors.)*

*(Just as he gets there, JAN enters, windblown, her jacket
pockets bulging. She moves slowly, in a contemplative
trance.)*

HARRY: You didn't kill yourself—

JAN: Neither did you.

HARRY: I worried.

JAN: Why not? What better do you have to do?

HARRY: Why were you gone so long? What were you
doing?

JAN: *(Taking a handful from her pocket)* I was collecting
seashells.... And thinking.

(HARRY looks out the downstage window.)

HARRY: This is not a good time for thinking. They're
coming back from their break—those workers in their
jeans with the union labels. The unwelcome mat is
being spread out before us. Gather ye mementoes and
exit while ye may.

*(Through much of the following he goes through the room
picking up books and papers and making a pile of them on
the table. He is very busy. JAN is very still.)*

JAN: What are you planning to wear?

HARRY: For what?

JAN: For our exit.

HARRY: I hadn't thought about it.

JAN: I think we should go naked. Give 'em a picture no paper will print.

HARRY: One will.

JAN: True. It's an irresistible story: "Naked Grandma and Grandpa Evicted from Ocean Cottage."

HARRY: "Grandma and Grandpa."

JAN: It's what we're going to be.

HARRY: Two decrepit homeless wandering old relics.

JAN: Two decrepit homeless wandering old relics who will never see their grandchild. I will never see my grandchild and will never see my son.

HARRY: We got over that—

JAN: You did. I didn't.

HARRY: He walked out—

JAN: You could have begged him not to go.

HARRY: That's not my style.

JAN: You could—just once—have begged—

HARRY: Never. If you cared so much, you could have gone off with him.

JAN: No, I couldn't.

HARRY: You could have found out where he was and gotten in touch.

JAN: And gone against you? Contacting Adam would have meant betraying you.

HARRY: You made a choice. Live with it.

JAN: But *not* contacting Adam meant betraying myself.... You tear me apart, you two.

HARRY: If he cared about you, he could have let you know how he was. But he didn't.

JAN: Perhaps he did. Perhaps he sent Frederica.

HARRY: I doubt it. She's an independent woman. She came on her own. Came, perhaps, to see if we had two heads, to see what her baby might inherit.

(The sound of the motor of heavy equipment is heard sporadically.)

They're manning their assault weapons. We'd better pull together anything we want—

JAN: When it comes, I want to see that baby!

HARRY: Go, for God's sake! Go and good riddance!

JAN: You know my first loyalty has always been to you.

HARRY: Except once.

JAN: Yes. Once.

HARRY: When you had those secret meetings with your student.

JAN: With my student.

HARRY: That one time—when you made it so clear you had something on the side.

JAN: Do you want to know the truth of it? God's truth?

HARRY: Oh, we're bringing God into it, are we? Then perhaps I will, after all these years, get a true confession.

JAN: ...I met the young man only once. And talked him into declaring his love for the girl of whom he was so fond.

HARRY: You.

JAN: Not me. More's the pity. He was young and handsome and I suspected you of wandering. I did meet that young boy with the intention of inflicting on him tea and sympathy. He'd have been a pushover. But I couldn't do it. That all-too-brief encounter only proved to me how ridiculously complete was my attachment to you.

HARRY: Then, all these years, these little hinted boasts of your infidelity—?

JAN: Were my best fiction.

(The heavy motor sound increases, stronger, more continuous than before.)

HARRY: Ah, the lies we perpetrate—to burnish our image with our uncommitted sins—

JAN: I know it will disgust you, at this late date, to hear it—but I was always faithful to you, Harry.

HARRY: You shouldn't have been. You should have had adventures!

JAN: Don't say that—

HARRY: You should have kicked up your heels and danced and wallowed with whomever you wanted whenever you liked!

JAN: You wouldn't say that if I had.

HARRY: You don't know—

JAN: *You* don't know. How I feel. What I'm thinking.

HARRY: I know what you were thinking on the beach. You were thinking about losing touch with Adam. That's what hurts you most, isn't it!

JAN: *(A breath, then—)* Yes.

HARRY: You had to choose between us and you chose me. You made a bad choice, old bean!

JAN: I didn't— ...I can't understand why you closed the door so firmly against Adam.

HARRY: *He* closed the door against *me!* Do you know how hard it is to live knowing your child hates you? Sometimes I think the only reason we have children is so there can be someone alive to confront us with our sins. To accuse us of every shortcoming, every deviation from the narrow. They can accuse! They don't know what's down the line! ...It's easy enough to judge others when you're at the beginning of the journey. When you're farther down the road you get some idea of how unexpectedly bumpy the trip can be.

JAN: I never understood—you wrote a negative review—and our son left us. Was his idea of ethical action so elevated—his sense of righteousness so intense—he had to leave?

HARRY: ...It wasn't that.

JAN: What was it?

HARRY: God's truth?

JAN: God's truth.

HARRY: (*After a long pause*) ...He saw me with Stone's wife. With Stone's young wife. Adam saw us together.

JAN: Stone's wife—?

HARRY: You didn't know—? About his wife and me?

JAN: No. I suspected there was someone. I had no idea it was her!

HARRY: Oh, yes. My betrayal of my mentor was more than words in a review. It was much more personal.

JAN: Stone's wife... But why—if this all happened back then—is everything exploding *now*?

HARRY: ...It seems, when Stone's wife moved out, she left behind some diaries. And this week, cleaning out a closet he'd never rummaged in before, Stone found them.

JAN: And in them he discovered the affair between the two of you.

HARRY: Yes.

JAN: So he did himself in because of an affair that happened years ago?

HARRY: Oh, no. People no longer kill themselves when they discover that their mate's been sleeping elsewhere. That's old-fashioned. In her diaries he discovered something that, to him, was far worse.

JAN: Go on.

HARRY: Are you sure you want to hear this?

JAN: Certain.

(There is the sound of motors revving up.)

HARRY: I'll tell you later.

JAN: Now. You'll tell me now.

HARRY *(A long pause. Then, finally)* ...It seems that, in her diary, Stone's wife boasted of how, in the very middle of the act of love, she'd told me about the passages which Stone had copied. She'd typed his manuscript for him. She knew from what obscure texts they had been copied down.

JAN: *(Laughing ironically)* So your identifying those passages wasn't based on esoteric knowledge of your own! It was based on inside information from Stone's wife, the woman with whom you were sleeping!

HARRY: It was her joke! A joke we shared together! Far more satisfying than what we shared between the sheets! We were making a fool of the great man! ...This week, when Stone at last discovered our collusion, it filled him with self-hatred and revulsion. He could bear her giving her body to another. In a sense, since she was much younger than he, that was almost to be expected. But for her to betray him by revealing to me the passages he'd copied, and for me to reveal that copying to the world based on inside information from her, that he could not bear. He wrote out the whole sordid tale in a long incoherent yet brilliant letter, fired it off to Cadwell—then shot himself.

JAN: Harry—

HARRY: He got me—after all these years, the old buzzard. Killed himself—and did me in with the same sword. The perfect drama, no, my love? Hamlet and Laertes rub each other out simultaneously—I do Stone in, he does in me!

JAN: No—Harry—. What you did was cruel, yes. But you felt you were being honest!

HARRY: Jan, wake up! I didn't damn his book out of unflinching intellectual honesty! I did it out of envy!

JAN: That's not true!

HARRY: It is! Let me, finally, at least be honest with *you*. I was trying to destroy him. I knew that no matter how many paragraphs Stone lifted from the works of others he would always be a giant, while I, no matter how many clever revelations of others' failings I managed to uncover, would always be a pygmy.

JAN: His theory was flawed!

HARRY: Don't you understand? I skewered his book out of pure unadulterated malice. By doing that, I proved his theory right!

JAN: Harry—!

HARRY: By damning his book out of malice I put a curse on myself and you and all our family. Since then, I haven't known a minute's peace, not one. *(He pauses. Spent)*

JAN: ...Why didn't you tell me this before?

HARRY: ...Because I was your hero.

JAN: My hero—

HARRY: I wanted to be that for you, but I botched it.

(The sound of heavy equipment being moved closer interrupts them.)

I'd better look around upstairs—to see if there's anything we might want to take.

(He exits up right.)

(Alone, JAN starts taking more shells out of her pockets. As she does so, she says to us, with growing wildness)

JAN: There's cockle shell, that's for remembrance. There's nautilus, that's to forget. I've been told something I do not want to know. How can I forget it? ...There's clam, that's to eat. ...Not raw. Unless you want to do yourself in. Why not? Why shouldn't we end it? Why shouldn't we let them scoop up our lifeless bodies with the detritus of our lives? *(She starts to sing)*
She wheeled a wheelbarrow
Through streets wide and narrow
'Twas there that I met
My sweet Molly Malone...
(Becoming increasingly disturbed) Harry says people no longer kill themselves when they discover that their mate's been sleeping elsewhere. Caring about such a thing—it's so—old-fashioned! *(Confused, upset)* Abalone shell, that's for ashtrays.... Levels of betrayal, mind and body. Mind *or* body. I pledge to thee the exclusive usage of my skin. I pledge to thee the eternal beauties of my true-blue mind. Blue, so very blue. *(Verging on breakdown)* Oyster shell, that's for finding pearls....

Pearls of wisdom. "This above all: To thine own self be
true." But isn't it selfish to be true only to one's self?
Isn't it a higher thing to be true to others? But which
other? My husband or my son? ...Adam. *(Wildly)*
Adam—! *(Attempting to control a growing hysteria)* Snail
shell, that's for making yourself go slowly, slowly....
Why did I stay? Out of love? Or was it vanity and
pride? The world observes thou hast a perfect love.
Do not shatter their illusions! ...But my husband was
brave, was he not?—to speak out honestly in print—
in spite of all, in spite of me? And did I not admire him
for daring all that honesty? Was it honesty? Or was it
malice—as he just now confessed? ...Lies! Thickets of
lies! How overgrown the paths get after a while! And
how narrow! How small the choice of roads one could
still take! *(She moves toward the glass doors which lead
to the sea.)* Nora walked out and slammed the door.
But she was younger! She deserted the field! I always
thought the honor was to stay! *(Singing)*
'Twas there that I met
My sweet Molly Malone...
(Keening. On the brink of madness) There's winkle. And
there's armadillo. There's turtle shell! Pull in your head!
You'll be safe at home! ...Safe... "When I am old and
gray and nodding by the fire... Remember how love
fled..." Yeats. Not Hawkesworth, loser of the Pulitzer.
I planned to sit by Harry's fire forever. I planned
freedom, him and me together. Not exile! I planned
light! Not this dark sky! I planned peace in this time
of my life—! *(Crying out in despair)* It was going to
be splendid! Not this.... In place of splendor—what?
Nothing. How do you go on loving—living—when
your world is over? *(Singing)*
Crying cockles and mussels
Alive Alive-O
Alive Alive-O
Alive Alive-O

Crying cockles and mussels
Alive...
(Spoken) Alive... *(Flatly)* Oh.

(HARRY has returned and heard the last verse, watching her, unobserved, with love and pity. JAN sees him. Quietly, she says)

JAN: And what am I supposed to do—now that I know all I know?

HARRY: You could leave me.

JAN: ...Make my way alone—without my only friend?

(A moment. HARRY breathes deeply then says, quietly, humbly)

HARRY: Jan, dear Jan—forgive? For flowers never sent, and diamonds never given, and beds never made, and lawns never mowed, for muffins never eaten, and jokes never laughed at... For tears never dried, and loveliness never complimented, for brilliance never acknowledged, and praises never sung, for devotion never recognized, and affection never valued... For hungers never satisfied, and joys never appreciated, for desires never gratified, and fidelities not treasured... For depths of soul and heights of spirit and moments of inexpressible beauty not sufficiently cherished... And for my betrayals—of mind and body—mentioned and unmentioned, forgive, pardon, grant absolution. *(He kneels at her feet.)* I am—so very sorry—that I've ditched our plane in the ocean and that you're drowning with me. Forgive. Please forgive me. *(He is weeping.)* I am so sorry...

(She holds him, comforts him for a time. Then, finally)

JAN: Don't be sorry.

HARRY: We flew higher than anybody, didn't we?

JAN: We did, my darling.

HARRY: Crossed oceans, crossed continents. You as my co-pilot. What a team we were.

JAN: ...What a team we *are*. *(She takes a shell out of her pocket.)* Look, Harry... Look what I found out by the jetty. *(She opens her hand.)* A shell. A perfect shell. An ordinary kind, but most unusual. No gull smashed inside it with his beak to extricate his dinner. Yet it's empty. Some sea creature must have just walked out of it to find a new home.

HARRY: Are you saying we could do that, too?

JAN: Listen... The sea. *(She puts the shell to his ear.)* Wherever we go, we can take it with us. Even if we are destroyed, there's comfort in knowing the ocean will never cease. It just renews itself, forever and always.

HARRY: Is that what saved you when you were walking by the water?

JAN: I was thinking about our grandchild, the child whom we will no doubt never see. There's hope in that young life. It makes the destruction of us that much easier to take. There'll be another wave on the beach when our wave is gone.

HARRY: Anne Lindbergh found comfort in shells.

JAN: ...Who's Anne Lindbergh?

(They exchange a smile. The sound of a bulldozer, approaching, becomes louder.)

HARRY: We'd better go.

JAN: Desert this shell and just move on?

HARRY: As quickly as we can.

(He starts picking up things and putting them in a duffel bag.)

(Suddenly, JAN says)

JAN: ... No. I have a better idea. Let's resist!

HARRY: What?

JAN: Barricade ourselves inside our fort and dare them to attack us!

HARRY: Why not? What have we got to lose? Let's do it!

JAN: No one shall say the Hawkesworths gave up without a fight!

HARRY: Come fire, come flood, come earthquake, come tornado! No one shall move us!

(The sound of the bulldozer becomes overwhelming.)

HARRY: They're almost at the porch!

JAN: They'll never dare to touch the house while we're still in it! Never! *(She calls out the window)* Go on! Attack! You don't dare, do you!

(The bulldozer's giant maw makes contact! There is the sound of wood smashing and crashing down. Debris falls from the hall ceiling. Suddenly brilliant daylight streams in from above left through the upstage opening.)

(HARRY goes to the entryway and looks, then says in disbelief)

HARRY: The front door is gone! The porch! The steps—! A gaping hole—!

(JAN and HARRY are taken aback at the reality of it.)

(We hear the bulldozer pull back and move around to the right of the house, revving up its motor to attack.)

JAN: They're moving around to attack us from the other side!

(JAN and HARRY are frozen, paralyzed. Heard clearly above the din, HARRY says)

HARRY: How do you go on when you can't go on? Where do you go when you have no place to go?

(For a moment they are completely lost.)

(As the sound of the bulldozer grows louder from stage right, FREDERICA suddenly appears from the left in the upstage opening. Bathed in its brilliant light, she says)

FREDERICA: Adam's here.... He wants to see you.

JAN: *(Joyously)* Adam—!

(JAN starts toward the opening then realizes HARRY has not moved. She turns back toward him and extends her hand.)

(HARRY says, with apprehension, yet with hope of reconciliation)

HARRY: Adam—

(HARRY takes JAN's hand and they exit through the rubble-filled upstage opening.)

(Illuminated in the opening, FREDERICA extends her hand in the direction of the off-stage reunion—and smiles.)

(Blackout)

END OF PLAY